JAAY EATS BY THE HANDFUL

Jaay-R Cook

Published by Denotion Research Group
Cover & Illustrations by TullipStudio

ISBN: 978-1-958634-00-4 (Paperback)
Printed in United States
1st Edition

This book is dedicated to my beautiful mother Audrey and my kids, especially to my daughter that is fighting one of life's greatest battles. I love you, Jaaymiree Cook!

Correct, Jaaymiree!
There are 5 main food groups-
one, two, three, four, five...

Who can name all 5 food groups?

Will someone share how much of each food group is considered healthy to eat? Feel free to look at our Food Power chart.

I use my hand to estimate how much food I should eat.

For some foods,
I use my whole fist.

One fist full of fruit or raw
vegetables is about one serving.

For most grains,
I use the front of my closed fist.
Or I use half of my whole fist.

Either of these is about one portion
of grains.

I use these motions for cooked
vegetables and beans too!

For meat, fish, and poultry,
I use the palm of my hand.

One portion of these proteins cover
one of my palms.

For most dairy foods,
I use my thumb.

A little more than one thumb size portion is one serving of dairy. This is also how I estimate a serving of nuts.

For liquids like fruit and vegetable juice,
I use one cupped hand for one portion.

But two cupped hands are used,
for one portion of milk and yogurt.

Oh wow, that's such an interesting approach to portioning your food, Jaay. Your dad sounds like an amazing personal trainer.Thanks for sharing with us!